THIRTY DAYS

An In-Depth Devotional

Edited by
Altagracia Alvarado
Katie Hoyer
Patricia Lyons
Elizabeth Panox-Leach

Foreword by
Judy Fentress Williams

Thirty Days
An In-Depth Daily Devotional

Volume One in the Thirty Days Series
An Experiment of TryTank@VTS and a publication of
Lifelong Learning at Virginia Theological Seminary

Cover photo: A waterfall in Fredon, New Jersey, USA
by Mark Hoyer

Interior illustrations by the Rev. Dr. Steve Thomason (stevethomason.net)

A record of this book is available from the Library of Congress.

ISBN: 9781312731585

FOREWORD

**"I believe that the books and stories we fall in love
with make us who we are, or not to claim too much,
the beloved tale becomes a part of
the way in which we understand things
and make judgments and choices in our daily lives."**[1]

I was somewhere around page 152 of The Lion the Witch and the
Wardrobe when I realized that Aslan was more than a lion! In that
moment the magical land of Narnia became quite real. Over the years,
I've read and re-read all seven volumes in the Chronicles of Narnia.
Sometimes I read the first volume, or the fifth or the seventh – it all
depended on what I was looking for. The story was doing something
more than entertaining me – it was not "merely a story told but a
reality lived."[2] I didn't have the language for it at the time, but I was
experiencing the power of certain kinds of stories, namely myth, to shape
and reinforce identity. When a young boy came home after a difficult
day and said to his mother, "I need to read the last Harry Potter book
again," he was looking for the assurance from the "old, old, story"[3] that
in the end, everything would be alright. Northrop Frye defines myth as a
story, "a narrative sequence" or "plot," that tells us what is most true.[4]

Modern day myths, like the old ones, have a particular function, namely to give shape to the world and help us to determine who we are in it.

Like the ancient myths, there are contemporary stories that remind us of what is most important, and why. We wrestle with essential questions about our existence in places like Wakanda, Middle Earth, Hogwarts and Tatooine. We delve into the complexities of humanity with creatures that are not human or are more than human and reflect on our world in other- worldly venues. Along with the characters, the readers embark on a journey that is outward and inward. Away from the comforts of the known world, we try on different perspectives as our narrative companions confront and seek to survive grief and achieve greatness. We embark on journeys to strange lands so we can come to terms with who we are and who we can become. We experience forgiveness and reconciliation. We are redeemed. Our hope is restored by a Wakandan Prince who steps into his destiny, and we find the courage to be authentically human because of a Wookie's love and friendship. An exquisite articulation of the afterlife comes in Gandalf's answer to Pippin's statement about death where he asserts, "the journey doesn't end here." In this sense, the new myths, like the old are stories that speak to those things we seek to understand. They are unavoidably theological. The reflections in this breviary are formed and informed by the beauty and power of these stories. If we are lucky, we will find ourselves, like the man in another ancient story saying, "Surely the LORD is in this place - and I did not know it."[5]

— *Judy Fentress-Williams*

1 Rushdie, Salman. "Ask Yourself Which Books You Truly Love," *The New York Times Sunday Review*, last modified May 24, 2021, https://www.nytimes.com/2021/05/24/opinion/sunday/salman-rushdie-world-literature.html.

2 Brevard Childs, Myth and Reality in the Old Testament (Eugene, OR: Wipf and Stock Publishers, 1962), 18.

3 "Tell Me the Old, Old Story" is the name of the poem by Katherine Hankey, later set to music as a hymn.

4 Northrop Frye, *The Great Code: The Bible and Literature* (And Diego: Harcourt Brace Jovanovich, Publishers, 1982), 32.

5 Genesis 28:16, New Revised Standard Version

How to use this DEVOTIONAL

From the Editors

1. Use it in whatever way or ways that bring you joy, learning and power.

2. The illustrated number drawings for each day are in black and white so that you can color them in if you wish. There is serious research in the past decade behind the thesis that coloring, doodling or illustrating ideas reduces stress and feds and heals the imagination. Get a marker or crayon and try it!

3. Feel free to engage any section of each day in any order you wish. The Editors designed this devotional believing that the question of the day (the section entitled "God's Will Be Done") is central. These questions guided our choices of quotations and prayers. If you want a consistent structure, try starting with the Gratitude Question in the upper left hand corner and working your way across and down!

4. There is some white space in the daily pages, as well as blank pages at the back of this book to record your thoughts or drawings that do not fit in the daily pages. Express yourself!

5. Not sure how to end your time with this devotional each day? Why not try to say out loud the printed prayer addressed to God? The editors wrote one-sentence prayers focusing on the ideas and verbs of the other sources for each day in order to ask God to do or be something specific in our lives. If you are new to the idea of talking directly to God, try it! Talking to God, with words or with our feelings that are too joyful, too painful, too mysterious or too deep for words, has changed the lives for the better of all editors of this book.

6. Please know that the people who put this book together were already praying for you as we began this work, and we have endeavored to pray for you whenever we see copies of this book in the world.

You are always held in prayer.

Giving Thanks

How can you express gratitude for the most valuable thing in your life today?

Epic Imagination

"But you know, happiness can be found even in the darkest of times, if one only remembers to turn on the light."

— Dumbledore,
J.K. Rowling's
*Harry Potter and the
Prisoner of Azkaban*

God's Will Be Done

Where have you found bliss in the last 24 hours?
Name it, and give thanks.

Hearing Voices

The fullness of Joy is to behold God in everything.

— **Julian of Norwich**

With joy they celebrated the festival of unleavened bread seven days; for the LORD had made them joyful, and had turned the heart of the king of Assyria to them, so that he aided them in the work on the house of God, the God of Israel.

Ezra 6:22

On Earth As It Is In Heaven

God of Bliss, enlighten me and ...

+ FURTHER IN

FURTHER UP

Giving Thanks

What was a turning point in your life – good, bad, or confusing – for which you are now grateful?

Epic Imagination

"No one answered. The noon-bell rang. Still no one spoke. Frodo glanced at all the faces, but they were not turned to him. All the Council sat with downcast eyes, as if in deep thought. A great dread fell on him, as if he was awaiting the pronouncement of some doom that he had long foreseen and vainly hoped might after all never be spoken. An overwhelming longing to rest and remain at peace by Bilbo's side in Rivendell filled all his heart. At last with an effort he spoke, and wondered to hear his own words, as if some other will was using his small voice.

'I will take the Ring,' he said, 'though I do not know the way.'"

— J.R.R. Tolkien's
The Fellowship of the Ring,
Book II, Chapter 2:
The Council of Elrond

God's Will Be Done

Reflect on your worship or church experiences. Where in those experiences have you felt God's presence?

Hearing Voices

"The fire has its flame and praises God. The wind blows the flame and praises God. In the voice we hear the word which praises God. And the word, when heard, praises God. So all of creation is a song of praise to God."

— Hildegard of Bingen

In the year that King Uzziah died, I saw the Lord sitting on a throne, high and lofty; and the hem of his robe filled the temple. Seraphs were in attendance above him; each had six wings: with two they covered their faces, and with two they covered their feet, and with two they flew.

And one called to another and said: "Holy, holy, holy is the LORD of hosts; the whole earth is full of his glory."

— Isaiah 6:1-3

On Earth As It Is In Heaven

God-with-us, show me ...

FURTHER UP + FURTHER IN

11

Giving Thanks

What is something that caught you off guard today,
and how did it make you uncomfortable or curious?

Epic Imagination

"Who are you?" asked Shasta.

"Myself," said the Voice, very deep and
low so that the earth shook: and again
"Myself," loud and clear and gay: and
then the third time "Myself," whispered
so softly you could hardly hear it, and yet
it seemed to come from all round you as if
the leaves rustled with it.

Shasta was no longer afraid that the Voice
belonged to something that would eat him,
nor that it was the voice of a ghost. But a
new and different sort of trembling came
over him. Yet he felt glad too.

C.S. Lewis' *The Horse and His Boy*
(The Chronicles of Narnia)

God's Will Be Done

How did you first learn about Jesus? What is your understanding of Jesus today? (Answer as honestly as possible!)

Hearing Voices

Many crowds followed him, and he cured all of them, and he ordered them not to make him known. This was to fulfill what had been spoken through the prophet Isaiah: "Here is my servant, whom I have chosen, my beloved, with whom my soul is well pleased. I will put my Spirit upon him, and he will proclaim justice to the Gentiles. He will not wrangle or cry aloud, nor will anyone hear his voice in the streets. He will not break a bruised reed or quench a smoldering wick until he brings justice to victory. And in his name the Gentiles will hope."

— Matthew 12:15b-21

On Earth As It Is In Heaven

God who came among us, awaken me to ...

Jesus of Nazareth is a troubling--and troublesome--figure, and it seems to me the church has never known what to do with him.

— Verna Dozier's *The Dream of God*

FURTHER UP + FURTHER IN

13

Giving Thanks

Where was your focus today? Were you aware of God's presence there?

Epic Imagination

"Your father and I would talk about this day all the time. He is with us. And it is your time to be king."

— Ramonda,
Ryan Coogler's *Black Panther*

God's Will Be Done

Think of your life. When did you feel close to God? When did you feel far away? What drew you close again?

Hearing Voices

Where can I go from your spirit?
Or where can I flee from your presence?
If I ascend to heaven, you are there;
if I make my bed in Sheol, you are there.
If I take the wings of the morning
and settle at the farthest limits of the sea,
even there your hand shall lead me,
and your right hand shall hold me fast.

— Psalm 139:7-10

There is no place in my soul, no corner of my character, where God is not.

— Evelyn Underhill

On Earth As It Is In Heaven

God from whom I cannot hide, draw me ...

FURTHER UP + FURTHER IN

15

Giving Thanks

When was the last time you went beyond your comfort zone?
What brought you there?

Epic Imagination

Finn: "We'll figure it out, we'll use the Force!"
Han Solo: "That's not how the Force works!"

J.J. Abrams' *The Force Awakens*

God's Will Be Done

When did you first read the Bible on your own? Why did that happen?

Hearing Voices

Then an angel of the Lord said to Philip, "Get up and go toward the south to the road that goes down from Jerusalem to Gaza." (This is a wilderness road.) So he got up and went. Now there was an Ethiopian eunuch, a court official of the Candace, queen of the Ethiopians, in charge of her entire treasury. He had come to Jerusalem to worship and was returning home; seated in his chariot, he was reading the prophet Isaiah. Then the Spirit said to Philip, "Go over to this chariot and join it." So Philip ran up to it and heard him reading the prophet Isaiah. He asked, "Do you understand what you are reading?" He replied, "How can I, unless someone guides me?" And he invited Philip to get in and sit beside him

— Acts 8:26-31

"My Dear Lucy, I wrote this story for you, but when I began it I had not realized that girls grow quicker than books. As a result you are already too old for fairy tales, and by the time it is printed and bound you will be older still. But some day you will be old enough to start reading fairy tales again."

— Dedication for C.S. Lewis'
The Lion, the Witch, and the Wardrobe
(The Chronicles of Narnia)

On Earth As It Is In Heaven

God of mystery, call me to ...

+ FURTHER IN

FURTHER UP

17

Giving Thanks

What is the last thing that someone shared with you?
How did you express gratitude for it?

Epic Imagination

Rubeus Hagrid: "I am what I am, an' I'm not ashamed. 'Never be ashamed,' my ol' dad used ter say, 'there's some who'll hold it against you, but they're not worth botherin' with.'"

J.K. Rowling's *Harry Potter and the Goblet of Fire*

God's Will Be Done

Write a thank you post, note or email to someone who helps you know and love yourself.

Hearing Voices

LORD, you have searched me out and known me; *
    you know my sitting down and my rising up;
    you discern my thoughts from afar.

You trace my journeys and my resting-places *
    and are acquainted with all my ways.

Indeed, there is not a word on my lips, *
    but you, O LORD, know it altogether.

— Psalm 139:1-3

"The more we let God take us over, the more truly ourselves we become – because He made us. He invented us. He invented all the different people that you and I were intended to be. . .It is when I turn to Christ, when I give up myself to His personality, that I first begin to have a real personality of my own."

— C.S. Lewis

On Earth As It Is In Heaven

God who knows me, thank you for ...

FURTHER UP + FURTHER IN

Giving Thanks

What is helping me to resist the urge to "do it all" today?

Epic Imagination

"Then an old wife, Ioreth, the eldest of the women who served in that house, looking on the fair face of Faramir, wept, for all the people loved him. And she said: 'Alas! if he should die. Would that there were kings in Gondor, as there were once upon a time, they say! For it is said in old lore: The hands of the king are the hands of a healer. And so the rightful king could ever be known.'

And Gandalf, who stood by, said: 'Men may long remember your words, Ioreth! For there is hope in them."

J.R.R. Tolkien's *The Return of the King, Book V, Chapter 8: The Houses of Healing (The Lord of the Rings)*

God's Will Be Done

What is your favorite piece of Scripture? Why do you love it?

Hearing Voices

Blessed Lord, who caused all holy Scriptures to be written for our learning: Grant us so to hear them, read, mark, learn, and inwardly digest them, that we may embrace and ever hold fast the blessed hope of everlasting life, which you have given us in our Savior Jesus Christ; who lives and reigns with you and the Holy Spirit, one God, for ever and ever. Amen.

— **The Book of Common Prayer, 1979**

I will walk at liberty,
      because I study your commandments.

I will tell of your decrees before kings
      and will not be ashamed.

I delight in your commandments,
      which I have always loved.

I will lift up my hands to your commandments,
      and I will meditate on your statutes.

— **Psalm 119:45-48**

On Earth As It Is In Heaven

God of many voices, help me to meditate on ...

+ FURTHER IN

FURTHER UP

21

Giving Thanks

How can you express gratitude for the most valuable thing in your life today?

Epic Imagination

"Peter, Adam's Son," said Father Christmas.

"Here, sir," said Peter.

"These are your presents," was the answer, "and they are tools not toys. The time to use them is perhaps near at hand. Bear them well." With these words he handed to Peter a shield and a sword. The shield was the color of silver and across it there ramped a red lion, as bright as a ripe strawberry at the moment when you pick it. The hilt of the sword was of gold and it had a sheath and a sword belt and everything it needed, and it was just the right size and weight for Peter to use. Peter was silent and solemn as he received these gifts, for he felt they were a very serious kind of present."

C. S. Lewis' *The Lion, the Witch and the Wardrobe (The Chronicles of Narnia)*

God's Will Be Done

How did you discover your gifts? How do they help you connect to others?

Hearing Voices

"Every creature is a glittering, glistening mirror of Divinity... With nature's help, humankind can set into creation all that is necessary and life sustaining."

— Hildegard of Bingen

"One of his disciples, Andrew, Simon Peter's brother, said to him, "There is a boy here who has five barley loaves and two fish. But what are they among so many people?"

— John 6:8-9

On Earth As It Is In Heaven

God who gives all gifts, strengthen me to use mine for... ...

+ FURTHER IN

FURTHER UP

Giving Thanks

What was a turning point in your life — good, bad, or confusing — for which you are now grateful?

Epic Imagination

Ramonda: "Your father taught you all that warrior nonsense—but he also taught you how to think. Don't fight this war with guns."

Ryan Coogler's *Black Panther*

God's Will Be Done

Is there or has there been someone in your life who shares your faith tradition, values, or practices? When was your last conversation with that person?

Hearing Voices

In those days Mary set out and went with haste to a Judean town in the hill country, where she entered the house of Zechariah and greeted Elizabeth. When Elizabeth heard Mary's greeting, the child leaped in her womb. And Elizabeth was filled with the Holy Spirit and exclaimed with a loud cry, "Blessed are you among women, and blessed is the fruit of your womb. And why has this happened to me, that the mother of my Lord comes to me? For as soon as I heard the sound of your greeting, the child in my womb leaped for joy. And blessed is she who believed that there would be a fulfillment of what was spoken to her by the Lord."

And Mary said, "My soul magnifies the Lord..."

And Mary remained with her about three months and then returned to her home.

— Luke 1:38-46, 56

"Whenever I stuck fast and honestly confessed myself at fault, she would by no means rest content but would force me by fresh questions to point out to her which of many different solutions seemed to me the most probable."

— Jerome, speaking of Paula, from
*Praying with Passionate Women:
Mystics, Martyrs, and Mentors*
by Bridget Mary Meehan, p. 45

On Earth As It Is In Heaven

God of our ancestors, guide me to ...

FURTHER UP + FURTHER IN

25

Giving Thanks

What is something that caught you off guard today, and how did it make you uncomfortable or curious?

Epic Imagination

Dumbledore: "'Ah, music,' he said, wiping his eyes. 'A magic beyond all we do here!'"

J.K. Rowling's *Harry Potter and the Sorcerer's Stone*

God's Will Be Done

Is there a piece of music, art or film where you see or experience God? Have you ever shared that experience with anyone?

Hearing Voices

I waited patiently upon the LORD; *
  he stooped to me and heard my cry.

He lifted me out of the desolate pit, out of the mire and clay; *
  he set my feet upon a high cliff and made my
  footing sure.

He put a new song in my mouth,
a song of praise to our God; *
  many shall see, and stand in awe,
and put their trust in the LORD.

—Psalm 40:1-3

"Every element has a sound, an original sound from the order of God; all those sounds unite like the harmony from harps and zithers."

— Hildegard of Bingen

On Earth As It Is In Heaven

God of beauty, sing into my soul so that ...

+ FURTHER IN

FURTHER UP

27

Giving Thanks

Where was your focus today? Were you aware of God's presence there?

Epic Imagination

Galadriel: "You may learn something, and whether what you see be fair or evil, that may be profitable, and yet it may not. Seeing is both good and perilous."

J.R.R. Tolkien's *The Fellowship of the Ring, Book II, Chapter 7 (The Lord of the Rings)*

God's Will Be Done

Take a five-minute walk. What do you see? Who do you see?

Hearing Voices

When Jesus turned and saw them following,
he said to them, "What are you looking for?"
They said to him, "Rabbi" (which translated
means Teacher), "where are you staying?"
He said to them, "Come and see."

— John 1:38

Christ has no body now on earth but yours,
no hands but yours, no feet but yours;
yours are the eyes through which is to look
out Christ's compassion to the world; yours
are the feet with which he is to go about doing
good; yours are the hands with which he is to
bless men now.

— St. Teresa of Avila

On Earth As It Is In Heaven

God who sees, open my eyes to ...

FURTHER UP + FURTHER IN

Giving Thanks

When was the last time you went beyond your comfort zone? What brought you there?

Epic Imagination

Obi-Wan Kenobi: "You will find that many of the truths we cling to depend greatly on our own point of view."

Richard Marquand's *Star Wars: Episode VI - Return of the Jedi*

God's Will Be Done

Share something you see out of your window or on a screen with someone who can see it too. What was their reaction? Was there a gap between your perception and theirs?

Hearing Voices

"If a man wishes to be sure of the road he travels on, he must close his eyes and walk in the dark."

— St. John of the Cross

"Now it was Mary Magdalene, Joanna, Mary the mother of James, and the other women with them who told this to the apostles. But these words seemed to them an idle tale, and they did not believe them. But Peter got up and ran to the tomb; stooping and looking in, he saw the linen cloths by themselves; then he went home, amazed at what had happened."

— Luke 24:10-11

On Earth As It Is In Heaven

God of paradox, open my mind to ...

+ FURTHER IN

FURTHER UP

Giving Thanks

What is the last thing that someone shared with you? How did you express gratitude for it?

Epic Imagination

"There was nothing to be afraid of any more. Eustace was a terror himself now and nothing in the world but a knight (and not all of those) would dare to attack him. He could get even with Caspian and Edmund now--

But the moment he thought this he realized that he didn't want to. He wanted to be friends. He wanted to get back among humans and talk and laugh and share things. He realized that he was a monster cut off from the whole human race. An appalling loneliness came over him. He began to see that the others had not really been fiends at all. He began to wonder if he himself had been such a nice person as he had always supposed."

C.S. Lewis' *Toyage of the Dawn Treader (The Chronicles of Narnia))*

God's Will Be Done

Scroll through your Facebook, Twitter, Instagram, or other feeds. What are the themes of joy or concern? Where do you see or hear God in your feed?

Hearing Voices

For we are so preciously loved by God that we cannot even comprehend it. No created being can ever know how much and how sweetly and tenderly God loves them. It is only with the help of his grace that we are able to persevere in spiritual contemplation with endless wonder at his high, surpassing, immeasurable love which our Lord in his goodness has for us.

— Julian of Norwich

Then he said, "Jesus, remember me when you come into your kingdom." Jesus replied, "Truly I tell you, today you will be with me in paradise."

— Luke 23:42-43

On Earth As It Is In Heaven

God who connects us, help me to share ...

FURTHER UP + FURTHER IN

Giving Thanks

What is helping me to resist the urge
to "do it all" today?

Epic Imagination

T'Challa: "Now, more than ever, the illusions
of division threaten our very existence. We all
know the truth: more connects us than sepa-
rates us. But in times of crisis the wise build
bridges, while the foolish build barriers. We
must find a way to look after one another, as if
we were one single tribe."

Ryan Coogler's *Black Panther*

God's Will Be Done

Identify an issue in your community and seek out the perspectives of other community members. Name the wounds they share with you that need healing.

Hearing Voices

It seems so much easier in these days to live morally than to live beautifully. Lots of us manage to exist for years without ever sinning against society, but we sin against loveliness every hour of the day.

— Evelyn Underhill

The hour is coming, indeed it has come, when you will be scattered, each one to his home, and you will leave me alone. Yet I am not alone because the Father is with me. I have said this to you so that in me you may have peace. In the world you face persecution, but take courage: I have conquered the world!

— John 16:32

On Earth As It Is In Heaven

God of healing, make space in me to hear and hold ...

FURTHER UP

\+ FURTHER IN

Giving Thanks

How can you express gratitude for the most valuable thing in your life today?

Epic Imagination

Padme Amidala: "All mentors have a way of seeing more of our faults than we would like. It's the only way we grow."

George Lucas's
Star Wars: Episode II – Attack of the Clones)

God's Will Be Done

Reflect on your immediate, extended, and chosen family. Where are the wounds? Where is there healing? Where do you see or feel God moving in those relationships?

Hearing Voices

Jesus, knowing that the Father had given all things into his hands and that he had come from God and was going to God, got up from supper, took off his outer robe, and tied a towel around himself. Then he poured water into a basin and began to wash the disciples' feet and to wipe them with the towel that was tied around him. He came to Simon Peter, who said to him, "Lord, are you going to wash my feet?" Jesus answered, "You do not know now what I am doing, but later you will understand." Peter said to him, "You will never wash my feet." Jesus answered, "Unless I wash you, you have no share with me."

— John 13:4-5

"If you look for truth, you may find comfort in the end; if you look for comfort you will not get either comfort or truth only soft soap and wishful thinking to begin, and in the end, despair."

— C.S. Lewis

On Earth As It Is In Heaven

God whose truth is love, heal us from ...

+ FURTHER IN

FURTHER UP

37

Giving Thanks

What was a turning point in your life - good, bad, or confusing - for which you are now grateful?

Epic Imagination

Dumbledore: "It takes a great deal of bravery to stand up to our enemies, but just as much to stand up to our friends."

J.K. Rowling's *Harry Potter and the Sorcerer's Stone*

God's Will Be Done

Reflect on what you love about your communities, in person and/or online. What forces threaten what you love about the spaces where you live?

Hearing Voices

Jesus said, "Peace I leave with you; my peace I give to you. I do not give to you as the world gives. Do not let your hearts be troubled, and do not let them be afraid."

— John 14:27

The glory of God is the human person fully alive.

— Irenaeus

On Earth As It Is In Heaven

God who shields our joy, give me courage to ...

+ FURTHER IN

FURTHER UP

Giving Thanks

What is something that caught you off guard today, and how did it make you uncomfortable or curious?

Epic Imagination

Thorin Oakenshield: "If more of us valued food and cheer and song above hoarded gold, it would be a merrier world."

J.R.R. Tolkien's *The Hobbit, or There and Back Again*

God's Will Be Done

Reflect on what you love about where you work or volunteer. What realities suck joy out of that space?

Hearing Voices

"To love at all is to be vulnerable. Love anything and your heart will be wrung and possibly broken. If you want to make sure of keeping it intact you must give it to no one, not even an animal. Wrap it carefully round with hobbies and little luxuries; avoid all entanglements. Lock it up safe in the casket or coffin of your selfishness. But in that casket, safe, dark, motionless, airless, it will change. It will not be broken; it will become unbreakable, impenetrable, irredeemable. To love is to be vulnerable."

— C.S. Lewis

When it was evening on that day, the first day of the week, and the doors were locked where the disciples were, for fear of the Jews, Jesus came and stood among them and said, "Peace be with you."

— John 20:19

On Earth As It Is In Heaven

God who labors with us, release us from ...

+ FURTHER IN

FURTHER UP

Giving Thanks

Where was your focus today? Were you aware of God's presence there?

Epic Imagination

"When I look in your face I can't help believing all you say: but then that's just what might happen with a witch too. How are we to know you're a friend?"

"You can't know," said the girl. "You can only believe--or not."

C.S. Lewis' *Voyage of the Dawn Treader*
(The Chronicles of Narnia)

God's Will Be Done

Think of your friendships. What habits of yours or theirs undermine trust and love?

Hearing Voices

Then Jesus said to him, "Put your sword back into its place, for all who take the sword will die by the sword."

— **Matthew 26:52**

"Friendship is something that creates equality and mutuality, not a reward for finding equality or a way of intensifying existing mutuality."

— **Rowan Williams**

On Earth As It Is In Heaven

God of loving-kindness, help me to honor ...

+ FURTHER IN

FURTHER UP

Giving Thanks

When was the last time you went
beyond your comfort zone?
What brought you there?

Epic Imagination

T'Challa: "You were wrong! All of you were
wrong! To turn your backs on the rest of the
world! We let the fear of discovery stop us from
doing what is right. No more! I cannot stay
here with you. I cannot rest while he sits on the
throne. He is a monster of our own making. I
must take the mantle back. I must! I must right
these wrongs."

Ryan Coogler's *Black Panther*

God's Will Be Done

What fears tempt you to misuse your powers over others, even in small and petty ways?

Hearing Voices

"Why do we fast, but you do not see?
Why humble ourselves, but you do not notice?"
Look, you serve your own interest on your fast day,
and oppress all your workers.
Look, you fast only to quarrel and to fight
and to strike with a wicked fist.

— Isaiah 58:3-4

We cannot know whether or not we love God, although there are strong indications for recognizing that we do love God; but we can know whether we love our neighbor. And be certain that the more advanced you see you are in love for your neighbor, the more advanced you will be in the love of God.

— Teresa of Avila

On Earth As It Is In Heaven

God who conquers fear and death, make me bold to ...

+ FURTHER IN

FURTHER UP

Giving Thanks

What is the last thing that someone shared with you? How did you express gratitude for it?

Epic Imagination

Luke Skywalker: "No one's ever really gone."

Rian Johnson's *Star Wars: Episode VIII — The Last Jedi*

God's Will Be Done

Think of the last time you felt sad or lonely. What was at the root of that feeling or feelings?

Hearing Voices

Pray, even if you feel nothing, see nothing. For when you are dry, empty, sick or weak, at such a time is your prayer most pleasing to God, even though you may find little joy in it. This is true of all believing prayer.

— Julian of Norwich

The dead man came out, his hands and feet bound with strips of cloth and his face wrapped in a cloth. Jesus said to them, "Unbind him, and let him go."

— John 11:44

On Earth As It Is In Heaven

God of tenderness, tend my wounds from ...

FURTHER UP   + FURTHER IN

47

Giving Thanks

What is helping me to resist the urge
to "do it all" today?

Epic Imagination

Harry Potter: "I'm going to keep going until
I succeed — or die. Don't think I don't know
how this might end. I've known it for years."

J.K. Rowling's *Harry Potter and the Deathly Hallows*

God's Will Be Done

Reflect on your core values. What are the values that ground you enough to take risks? Is taking the time to rest ever a risk?

Hearing Voices

My, how busy we become when we lose sight of how God loves us.

— Julian of Norwich

When Jesus realized that they were about to come and take him by force to make him king, he withdrew again to the mountain by himself.

— John 6:15

On Earth As It Is In Heaven

God who is faithful, empower me to ...

+ FURTHER IN

FURTHER UP

Giving Thanks

How can you express gratitude for the most valuable thing in your life today?

Epic Imagination

Treebeard marched on, singing with the others for a while. But after a time his voice died to a murmur and fell silent again ... 'Of course, it is likely enough, my friends,' he said slowly, 'likely enough that we are going to our doom: the last march of the Ents. But if we stayed at home and did nothing, doom would find us anyway, sooner or later. That thought has long been growing in our hearts; and that is why we are marching now. It was not a hasty resolve. Now at least the last march of the Ents may be worth a song. Aye,' he sighed, 'we may help the other peoples before we pass away. Still, I should have liked to see the songs come true about the Entwives. I should dearly have liked to see Fimbrethil again. But there, my friends, songs like trees bear fruit only in their own time and their own way: and sometimes they are withered untimely."

J.R.R. Tolkien's *The Two Towers, Book III, Chapter 4: Treebeard (The Lord of the Rings)*

50

God's Will Be Done

Reflect on a time when you made a sacrifice to stand up for something or someone you believed in or felt called to defend?

Hearing Voices

"We shall awaken from our dullness and rise vigorously toward justice. If we fall in love with creation deeper and deeper, we will respond to its endangerment with passion."

— **Hildegard of Bingen**

"Why do you call me 'Lord, Lord,' and do not do what I tell you? I will show you what someone is like who comes to me, hears my words, and acts on them."

— Luke 6:46-47

On Earth As It Is In Heaven

God of mercy and justice, move me to ...

+ FURTHER IN

FURTHER UP

51

Giving Thanks

What was a turning point in your life — good, bad, or confusing —
for which you are now grateful?

Epic Imagination

"Now, Bree," he said, "you poor, proud,
frightened Horse, draw near. Nearer still,
my son. Do not dare not to dare. Touch me.
Smell me. Here are my paws, here is my tail,
these are my whiskers. I am a true Beast."

"Aslan," said Bree in a shaken voice,
"I'm afraid I must be rather a fool."

"Happy the Horse who knows that while he is
still young. Or the Human either."

C.S. Lewis' *The Horse and His Boy*
(The Chronicles of Narnia)

God's Will Be Done

Have you ever made a commitment that you now regret? What has changed in you that causes regret?

Hearing Voices

"I think that if God forgives us we must forgive ourselves. Otherwise, it is almost like setting up ourselves as a higher tribunal than Him."

— C.S. Lewis

If we say that we have no sin, we deceive ourselves, and the truth is not in us. If we confess our sins, he who is faithful and just will forgive us our sins and cleanse us from all unrighteousness.

— I John 1:8-9

On Earth As It Is In Heaven

God of repentance, forgive me for ...

FURTHER UP + FURTHER IN

53

Giving Thanks

What is something that caught you off guard today, and how did it make you uncomfortable or curious?

Epic Imagination

Okoye: "I am loyal to the throne. What are you loyal to?"

Ryan Coogler's *Black Panther*

God's Will Be Done

Reflect on a time when you made a public commitment. Have you remained faithful to it? How is it changing your life?

Hearing Voices

Jesus did not call human beings to worship him, but to follow him.

— Verna Dozier

While they were eating, he took a loaf of bread, and after blessing it he broke it, gave it to them, and said, "Take; this is my body."

— Mark 14:22

On Earth As It Is In Heaven

God who keeps promises, renew in me ...

FURTHER UP

+ FURTHER IN

55

Giving Thanks

Where was your focus today? Were you aware of God's presence there?

Epic Imagination

Luke Skywalker to Rey: "This is not going to go the way that you think."

Rian Johnson's *Star Wars: Episode VIII – The Last Jedi*

God's Will Be Done

Have you ever rejected a call from God? Would you reject that call today? Why or why not?

Hearing Voices

Since God commanded me to go, I must do it.

— **Joan of Arc**

Jesus said to them, "Truly I tell you, the tax collectors and the prostitutes are going into the kingdom of God ahead of you. For John came to you in the way of righteousness, and you did not believe him, but the tax collectors and the prostitutes believed him, and even after you saw it you did not change your minds and believe him."

— **Matthew 21:31-32**

On Earth As It Is In Heaven

God who gifts us with free will, show me ...

+ FURTHER IN

FURTHER UP

Giving Thanks

When was the last time you went beyond your comfort zone?
What brought you there?

Epic Imagination

Dumbledore: "Indifference and neglect often do much more damage than outright dislike."

J.K. Rowling's *Harry Potter and the Order of the Phoenix)*

God's Will Be Done

Greet at least one person today with intentionality and undivided attention. How does it feel?

Hearing Voices

"Every creature is a glittering, glistening mirror of Divinity."

— **Hildegard of Bingen**

"Because of the tender mercy of our God,
    the dawn from on high will break upon us,
to shine upon those who sit in darkness and in the shadow of death,
    to guide our feet into the way of peace."

— **Luke 1:78-79**

On Earth As It Is In Heaven

God who is always present, remind me that ...

+ FURTHER IN

FURTHER UP

Giving Thanks

What is the last thing that someone shared with you?
How did you express gratitude for it?

Epic Imagination

Haldir: "The world is indeed full of peril, and in it there are many dark places; but still there is much that is fair, and though in all lands love is now mingled with grief, it grows perhaps the greater."

J.R.R. Tolkien's *The Fellowship of the Ring, Book II, Chapter 6: Lothlórien (The Lord of the Rings))*

God's Will Be Done

Perform a simple act of intentional love today. If asked why, answer authentically.

Hearing Voices

Act, and God will act.

— Joan of Arc

You show me the path of life.
In your presence there is fullness of joy;
in your right hand are pleasures forevermore.

— Psalm 16:11

On Earth As It Is In Heaven

God of loving intention, challenge me to ...

FURTHER UP + FURTHER IN

61

Giving Thanks

What is helping me to resist the urge to "do it all" today?

Epic Imagination

Lucy woke out of the deepest sleep you can imagine, with the feeling that the voice she liked best in the world had been calling her name.

C.S. Lewis' *Prince Caspian (The Chronicles of Narnia)*

God's Will Be Done

Take time today to dwell in your love for and thoughts of five people in your life.

Hearing Voices

Love is creative. It does not flow along the easy paths, spending itself in the attractive. It cuts new channels, goes where it is needed.

— Evelyn Underhill

As the Father has loved me, so I have loved you; abide in my love. If you keep my commandments, you will abide in my love, just as I have kept my Father's commandments and abide in his love. I have said these things to you so that my joy may be in you, and that your joy may be complete. This is my commandment, that you love one another as I have loved you. No one has greater love than this, to lay down one's life for one's friends.

— John 15:9-13

On Earth As It Is In Heaven

God who is near to us, abide in me so that ...

FURTHER UP + FURTHER IN

Giving Thanks

How can you express gratitude for the most valuable thing in your life today?

Epic Imagination

Nakia: "You can't let your father's mistakes define who you are. You get to decide what kind of king you are going to be."

Ryan Coogler's *Black Panther*

God's Will Be Done

Flip back to the first day of this book. What are the gaps between your answers then and now?

Hearing Voices

"Relying on God has to begin all over again every day as if nothing had yet been done."

— **C.S. Lewis,** *Letters to Malcolm: Chiefly on Prayer*

"An argument arose among them concerning which one of them was the greatest. But Jesus, aware of their inner thoughts, took a little child and put it by his side and said to them, "Whoever welcomes this child in my name welcomes me, and whoever welcomes me welcomes the one who sent me, for the least among all of you is the greatest."

— **Luke 9:46-48**

On Earth As It Is In Heaven

God of growth, transform in me ...

+ FURTHER IN

FURTHER UP

Giving Thanks

What was a turning point in your life — good, bad, or confusing —
for which you are now grateful?

Epic Imagination

Luke Skywalker to Rey: "Confronting fear is the destiny of the
Jedi. Your destiny."

J.J. Abrams' *Star Wars: Episode IX – The Rise of Skywalker*

God's Will Be Done

Use this QR code to read the Baptismal Covenant in the Book of Common Prayer. Is there any part of it that you feel called to commit to in any way? What would be your next step?

Hearing Voices

Faith is not a refuge from reality. It is a demand that we face reality ... The true subject matter of religion is not our own little souls, but the Eternal God and His whole mysterious purpose, and our solemn responsibility to Him.

— Evelyn Underhill

He has shown strength with his arm;
>   he has scattered the proud in the
>   imagination of their hearts.
He has brought down the powerful from their thrones
>   and lifted up the lowly ...

— Luke 1:51-52 8

On Earth As It Is In Heaven

God of hope, walk with me towards ...

+ FURTHER IN

FURTHER UP

Pages for Reflection

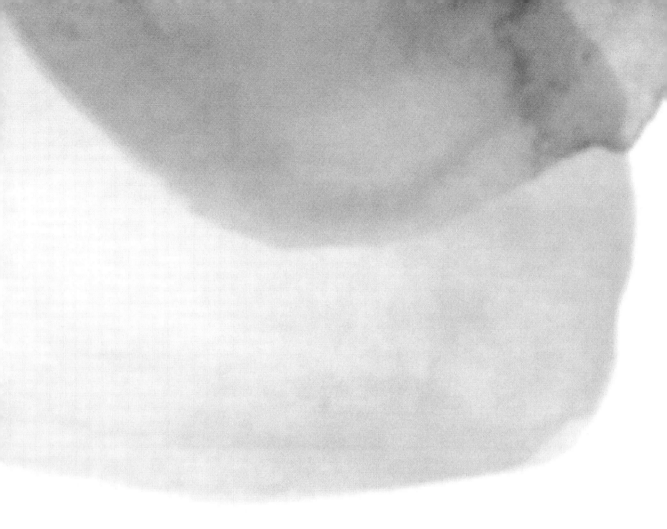

78

79

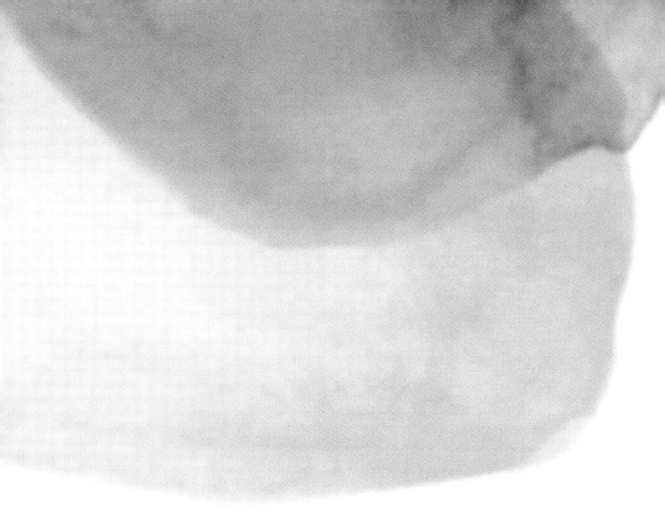

88

89

Why This Stuff Works

C.S. Lewis once wrote that looking at our current confusing and broken world is like looking at the back of a traditional oriental rug, where one sees only endless knots and chaotic splashes of color without any clear design or discernable pattern. But, offered Lewis, Christian faith teaches that at our death and resurrection into eternal life and into complete truth, our perception will be perfected, and we will experience an awareness of all things like looking at the other side of a rug's knotted chaos. Christian hope is that we will see the intended beauty of all creation. This perfected perception when it comes will not erase our formation and wisdom from our particular joys and wounds from human life, but rather we will 'know fully as we are fully known' that the beatific vision was gathered and grown from knots and chaos. The imagination of the Book of Genesis tells us that God began all creation making matter out of a formless void. I have not ever thought that Lewis was saying that any future perfected perspective justifies or explains why humans delight or suffer as we do. His point to me was to declare the belief in Divine intended beauty as undefeated by human freedom and its potentially destructive power. I have never forgotten his metaphor and its role to remind me that many things we see now are far more complicated and perhaps more designed for love, joy, and resurrection than we could ever imagine. As the New Testament declares, 'Now we see through a glass dimly, but then we shall see face to face.'

If you have made it to this page in this devotional book, perhaps I can tempt you to read just a few paragraphs more. I want to turn over the oriental rug and share the intentional faith-deepening design of this book, both so that you can see why we chose the words and images we did but also to explain why you may, by God's grace, have felt something change, something shift, or something sing in your mind or heart. There were multiple structures of learning theory and faith development models that guided all the choices we made for words and images on each page. We relied on current research about game theory, stress reduction strategies using story and drawing, frameworks for feeding the human imagination's longing for epic meaning and journeys, and growth models for deepening one's faith and hope.

We aimed to lead you through five stages of spiritual reflection, using a question for the day. Questions on Days 1-10 were meant to draw the reader's attention INWARD, reflecting on where we find God in ourselves and in the world. Questions 11-15 were an invitation to LOOK AROUND, to see what God is doing and what God's work is stirring in us. Questions on Days 16-20 focused on the forces of darkness or destruction we encounter every hour and how we are or are trying to

RENOUNCE those levers against light that are renounced in Baptismal Vows. Questions on Days 21-25 invited thoughts and ideas about COMMITMENT, about how we respond to our awareness of God with our whole selves. Questions on Days 26-30 pointed OUTWARD, inviting readers to dream and dare to live out faith in the world.

The gratitude sections were modeled on 'The Way of Love,' which is a set of faith practices written and taught in the Episcopal Church. Those practices are summarized in seven verbs: Turn, Learn, Pray, Worship, Bless, Go, and Rest. The gratitude section for each day in this devotional was rooted in one of these seven, starting on Day One with 'turn,' Day Two focusing on 'learn,' etc. Every seven days, the devotional would return to 'turn,' and move through the seven practices again. The goal was to meditate on and grow into these practices that are planted in us and made possible by the Holy Spirit. We thought that gratitude was a good place to start when building spiritual muscle.

Lastly, we wanted this Thirty Days to be modeled on something called 'The Catechumenate,' which means the process of preparing for the Sacrament of Baptism. We have records to show that the ancient followers of Jesus Christ were practicing this method to prepare for Baptism as early as the 3rd and 4th centuries.

I do not know where you are in your spiritual journey. Some of you are most likely not baptized and don't think much about it at all, if ever. Others of you are baptized and it is meaningful to you. And still others of you are simply seeking an understanding of what baptism might mean. No matter where you are, we thought that using this ancient and powerful form of preparation for a deeper spiritual life was a good framework for any daily devotional.

Too often baptism, in contemporary practice, is merely a scheduled event rather than initiation into a radical new life, oriented towards God and God's purposes. Through regular experiences of reflecting on worship and scripture, through fellowship, prayer, and active engagement in ministry, Christians of all ages and abilities become disciples marked for mission, God's mission, in the world.

Most of us are looking for a God who is too small and too tame … What does this tell us about the power of baptism? The awesome dynamism of God the Spirit should lead us to ask ourselves with what kind of expectation and anticipation do we prepare for baptism, whether our own, or that of someone we love? Do we really expect to be shaken to the foundations? Do we really expect to change? Are we willing to discover that volcanic inferno beneath everydayness? Most often, I suspect we are not."

– Marianne Micks, Theologian and Professor

The catechumenate is a process that guides and supports people into Christian life and practice as they respond to the movement of God in their lives. It is not a program. It is a journey, often described as The Way, the way of living into conversion into Christ, the way of entering into the Body of Christ, the way of preparing for baptism, the way of discerning one's God-given vocation, all with the support of other Christians in community.

"All who have been baptized by water and the Holy Spirit are called to ministry "far beyond the walls of any church building. They are Christ's ambassadors to the world. They are agents of good."

– Marianne Micks

The catechumenate might best be understood as apprenticeship into faith in Christ. It is both very ancient and timeless. Its pattern is drawn from the Exodus and the Paschal Mystery of the dying and rising of Christ. These two historic narratives define the nature of our human relationship with God, our journeys from exile to adoption, of being converted and ultimately entering life in Christ. Its practice is lived out in the dynamics of worshiping congregations that follow the liturgical year, attentive to the movement of the Holy Spirit through text, tradition, and transforming moments of everyday life.

In the current Episcopal liturgy to begin the catechumenate in a community, the first words of the service ask the catechumens to answer a question in front of everyone: "What do you seek?" Preparing for baptism is not a process to put things into you that you do not already have. Preparing for baptism is to call out the deepest longings in you that you carry and have carried for life. It is a response to human longings, not a source of it. This Thirty Day Devotional assumes that you have deep spiritual longings and a powerful spiritual imagination. Our hope was that this devotional asked you, in ways as diverse as possible, "what do you seek?" Our prayer is that along the Thirty Day journey you heard whispers or maybe even sirens from God that speak to your longings and offer them hope, fulfillment, and the joy of abundant life.

On behalf of the Editors, I pray that you have enjoyed the experience of The Thirty Days. And I mean literally 'enjoyed,' since the roots of that word mean to 'give joy to' or 'rejoice.' In the Christian tradition, joy is not the same as happiness. Happiness is a feeling, a mood, a state of being or state of mind. And it's great. But joy is something more. Joy causes happiness. Joy can also cause tears. Joy can cause feelings of guilt. Joy can cleanse. Joy can heal. Joy can liberate. Joy is not a feeling; it is a cause of feelings and experiences. Joy is a root, not a fruit. Joy belongs to God. Joy is part of God's language to us and to all creation. It is not our own feelings. It is not our own thoughts. Joy comes to us and dwells with us for a time. Christians believe that at the end of time, all creation will be in joy forever. God makes it and shares it. And when it happens to us, we are changed. Always.

— *Patricia Lyons*

ABOUT THE EDITORS

Altagracia Alvarado is the Coordinator of Christian Formation and Discipleship Resources in Lifelong Learning at Virginia Theological Seminary. Her undergraduate studies explored the role of arts-based education in honoring the shared histories of the African diaspora and catalyzing Black liberation and healing. She is an herbalist, doula, and prose poet who is passionate about the potential of practical mysticism as a foundation for intergenerational Christian formation.

Katie Hoyer is a member of the class of 2023 at Virginia Theological Seminary, where she is currently a music teaching assistant, a seminarian at Christ Episcopal Church in Rockville, MD, and a candidate for Holy Orders in the Episcopal Diocese of Massachusetts. Katie's Christian formation is rooted in a multigenerational family, The Episcopal Church, liturgical and congregational singing, interfaith relationships, and a lifelong love of Narnia and Middle Earth.

Patricia "Tricia" Lyons, D.Min. is a senior lecturer and an affiliated faculty member at Virginia Theological Seminary. Tricia is also senior advisor to the Dean for evangelism initiatives. Her baptismal imagination is constantly being formed for joy, courage, and hope from reading, writing, and preaching about epic narratives and following Jesus in the world. She believes evangelism is how we set the powers of baptism free.

Elizabeth Panox-Leach is the Manager of Digital and External Affairs for Lifelong Learning at Virginia Seminary. She has spent her career in communications serving the needs of the community, both in the public sector and on behalf of The Episcopal Church. An Episcopal Communicators board member and cradle Episcopalian, Elizabeth lives in Washington, DC.

Judy Fentress-Wiliams, Ph.D. is professor of Old Testament at Virginia Theological Seminary. Her fields of expertise include Hebrew Bible, dialogic interpretation, religious studies, Afro-American studies, and literary criticism. She also has interests in fantasy/comic literature and film. Her most recent publication is "Holy Imagination: A Literary and Theological Introduction to the Whole Bible."

NOTES ON CONTRIBUTORS

Josh Hosler, curator of our Narnia quotations, is rector of The Episcopal Church of the Good Shepherd in Federal Way, WA. He has worked in youth, campus, and camp ministries as well as congregational settings as both a lay person and now an ordained person. He is a master of C.S. Lewis' life and works and a Narnia maven.

Katie Hoyer, curator of our Lord of the Rings quotations, is a member of the class of 2023 at Virginia Theological Seminary, where she is currently a teaching assistant for music, seminarian at Christ Episcopal Church in Rockville, MD, and candidate for Holy Orders in the Episcopal Diocese of Massachusetts. Katie is a firm believer in elevenses.

Greg Milikin, curator of our Star Wars quotations, is rector of Grace Episcopal Church in New Lenox, IL. Before ordination, Greg spent over ten years working in the film industry, primarily at Fox Searchlight Pictures. Greg is the author of "Being Called, Being Gay," a primer for the LGBTQIA+ community discerning for ministry in the Episcopal Church.

Jason Prati, curator of our Harry Potter quotations, is rector of All Saints Episcopal Church in New Albany, Ohio. Fr. Jason is a former Roman Catholic Priest. His 20 years in ordained ministry have involved school chaplaincy, parish ministry, diocesan formation of new clergy, teaching liturgy, forming an intentional community and pastoral care of seminarians. Fr. Jason's office has more Harry Potter swag than Universal Studios.

Shayna Watson, curator of our Black Panther quotations, is canon pastor at St. Stephen's Episcopal Cathedral in Harrisburg, PA. As a community activist, she has a track record of organizing community events and fundraisers, facilitating anti-racism and cultural sensitivity platforms, and developing innovative ways to converse about challenging topics. Shayna is fed by epic narratives in comics and film and organized the groundbreaking "TheoCon," a conference at Virginia Seminary, focused on the intersection of theology and fantasy literature and pop culture.

Made in the USA
Middletown, DE
12 April 2023

28706792R00064